Step Out

Advisory Panel

Sharon Adams
Marilyn Bailey
Sue Evans
Demetra Georgopoulous
Nancy Leonard
Linda Miller
Miriam Trehearne

Senior Program Consultant

Jennette MacKenzie

Program Consultant

Christine Finochio

I(T)P Nelson

an International Thomson Publishing company

Toronto • Albany • Bonn • Boston • Cincinnati • Detroit • London • Madrid • Melbourne
Mexico City • New York • Pacific Grove • Paris • San Francisco • Singapore • Tokyo • Washington

I(T)P® International Thomson Publishing

The ITP logo is a trademark under licence
www.thomson.com

© Copyright 1999 ITP®Nelson

Published by
I(T)P® Nelson

A division of Thomson Canada Limited
1120 Birchmount Road
Scarborough, Ontario M1K 5G4
www.nelson.com

Printed and bound in Canada
 2 3 4 5 6 7 8 9 0/ML/7 6 5 4 3 2 1 0 9

Canadian Cataloguing in Publication Data

Main entry under title:

Nelson language arts

Contents: (v.1) Step out – (v.2) Reach out – (v.3) Leap out
ISBN 0-17-618557-7 (v.1) ISBN 0-17-618558-5 (v.2) ISBN 0-17-618559-3 (v.3)

1. Readers (Primary). I. Title: Nelson language arts 2.

| PE1119.N443 1998 | 428.6 | C98-932551-2 |

Executive Editor: Susan Green
Project Editor: Anne-Marie Wallace
Production Coordinator: Theresa Thomas
Art Direction and Design: Peggy Rhodes, Sylvia Vander Schee and Suzanne Peden
Permissions: Jill Young and Karen Taylor
Equity Consultant: Ken Ramphal

Table of Contents

Visiting Aunt Zelda 4

A List 8

How to Be a Friend 22

I Have a Friend 23

The Enormous Potato 24

Whoever You Are 36

Tsimshian Carver 44

Computers at Work 50

A Supermarket Song 56

The "Quiet" Rule 58

Canada's Creatures 64

The Paper Crane 72

Sidewalk Sticks 80

Mary Margaret's Tree 84

Visiting Aunt Zelda

By Jeanne Modesitt

Dear Mom and Dad,
I hope you are having a fun time in Europe.
Aunt Zelda and I are getting along great.
Whoever told you that Aunt was a bit ... well,
strange couldn't have been more wrong. Aunt
Zelda and I do all sorts of fun, normal
things together like ...

take her pets on walks,

go bike ridir

fly kites,

bake cookies,

learn new skills,

get our hair cut,

go for drives,

dress up,

6

roller-skate,

and play cards.

As you can see, Aunt Zelda is the perfect sitter for me. In fact, right after I finish this letter, we're going to try out this new science toy that we just finished building. I'm sure it will be a blast!

Sincerely yours,
Drew

7

A List

By Arnold Lobel

One morning Toad sat in bed.
"I have many things to do," he said.
"I will write them
all down on a list
so that I can remember them."
Toad wrote on a piece of paper:

A List of things to do today

Then he wrote:

Wake up

"I have done that," said Toad,
and he crossed out:

~~Wake up~~

Then Toad wrote other things
on the paper.

A List
of things to do
today

~~Wake up~~
Eat Breakfast
Get Dressed
Go to Frog's House
Take walk with Frog
Eat lunch
Take nap
Play games with Frog
Eat Supper
Go To Sleep

"There" said Toad.
"Now my day
is all written down."
He got out of bed
and had something to eat.
Then Toad crossed out:

~~Eat Breakfast~~

Toad took his clothes
out of the closet
and put them on.
Then he crossed out:

~~Get Dressed~~

Toad put the list in his pocket.

He opened the door and walked
out into the morning.
Soon Toad was at Frog's front door.
He took the list from his pocket
and crossed out:

Go to Frog's House

Toad knocked at the door.

"Hello," said Frog.

"Look at my list
of things to do,"
said Toad.

"Oh," said Frog,
"that is very nice."

Toad said, "My list tells me
that we will go
for a walk."

"All right," said Frog.
"I am ready."

Frog and Toad
went on a long walk.
Then Toad took the list
from his pocket again.
He crossed out:

~~Take walk with Frog~~

Just then there was a strong wind.
It blew the list
out of Toad's hand.
The list blew high up
into the air.

"Help!" cried Toad.
"My list is blowing away.
What will I do without my list?"

"Hurry!" said Frog.
"We will run and catch it."

"No!" shouted Toad.
"I cannot do that."

"Why not?" asked Frog.

"Because," wailed Toad,
"running after my list
is not one of the things
that I wrote
on my list of things to do!"

Frog ran after the list.
He ran over hills and swamps,
but the list blew on and on.
At last Frog came back to Toad.
"I am sorry," gasped Frog,
"but I could not catch
your list."

"Blah," said Toad.

"I cannot remember any of the things
that were on my list of things to do.
I will just have to sit here
and do nothing," said Toad.
Toad sat and did nothing.
Frog sat with him.

After a long time Frog said,
"Toad, it is getting dark.
We should be going to sleep now."

"Go to sleep!' shouted Toad.
"That was the last thing on my list!"
Toad wrote on the ground with a stick:

Go to sleep

Then he crossed out:

~~Go to sleep~~

"There," said Toad.
"Now my day
is all crossed out!"

"I am glad," said Frog.

Then Frog and Toad
went right to sleep.

How to Be a Friend

By Pat Lowery Collins

Keep a secret
Tell a wish
Listen
to
a dream

I Have a Friend

By Karla Kuskin

I have a friend who keeps on
   standing on her hands.
That's fine,
Except I find it very difficult to
   talk to her
Unless I stand on mine.

The Enormous Potato

By Aubrey Davis

There once was a farmer who had an eye.
It wasn't like your eye or my eye.
It was a potato eye.
The farmer planted it.
And it grew into a potato.

The potato grew bigger and bigger.
It grew fat.
It grew enormous.
It was the biggest potato in the world.

"It's time to pull it out,"
said the farmer.
So he grabbed the potato.
He pulled and pulled again.
But the potato wouldn't
come out of the ground.
So he called his wife.

WIFE! YOO-HOO! WIFE!

The wife grabbed the farmer.
The farmer grabbed the potato.
They pulled and pulled again.
But the potato wouldn't
come out of the ground.
So the wife called their daughter.

DAUGHTER! OH, DAUGHTER!

The daughter grabbed the wife.
The wife grabbed the farmer.
The farmer grabbed the potato.
They pulled and pulled again.
But the potato wouldn't
come out of the ground.
So the daughter called the dog.

"ROWF! ROWF! ROWF!"
The dog grabbed the daughter.
The daughter grabbed the wife.
The wife grabbed the farmer.
The farmer grabbed the potato.
They pulled and pulled again.
But the potato wouldn't
come out of the ground.
So the dog called the cat.

COME, CAT! COME!

"MEOW! MEOW! MEOW!"
The cat grabbed the dog.
The dog grabbed the daughter.
The daughter grabbed the wife.
The wife grabbed the farmer.
The farmer grabbed the potato.
They pulled and pulled again.
But the potato wouldn't
come out of the ground.
So the cat called the mouse.

"SQUEAK! SQUEAK! SQUEAK!"

The mouse grabbed the cat.
The cat grabbed the dog.
The dog grabbed the daughter.
The daughter grabbed the wife.
The wife grabbed the farmer.
The farmer grabbed the potato.
They pulled and pulled again.

RRRRRRRRRRRRRRRRRRRRRR ... RIP!

Out came the potato!

"That's a big potato!" said the farmer.
"That's a big potato!" said the wife.
"That's a dirty potato!" said the daughter.
So they washed it, and chopped it,
and cooked it, too.

The smell of potato brought the people from town.
They brought forks.
They brought bowls.
They brought butter and salt.

Soon everyone was eating potato.
My, it was good.
They ate and they ate ...
till the potato was gone.
And now the story is gone, too.

Whoever You Are

By Mem Fox

Little one,
whoever you are,
wherever you are,
there are little ones
just like you
all over the world.

Their skin may be
different from yours,
and their homes may be
different from yours.

Their schools may be
different from yours,
and their lands may be
different from yours.

Their lives may be
different from yours,
and their words may be
very different from yours.

But inside,
their hearts are
just like yours,
whoever they are,
wherever they are,
all over the world.

Their smiles are like yours,
and they laugh just like you.
Their hurts are like yours,
and they cry like you, too,
whoever they are,
wherever they are,
all over the world.

Little one,
when you are older
and when you are grown,
you may be different,
and they may be different,
wherever you are,
wherever they are,
in this big, wide world.

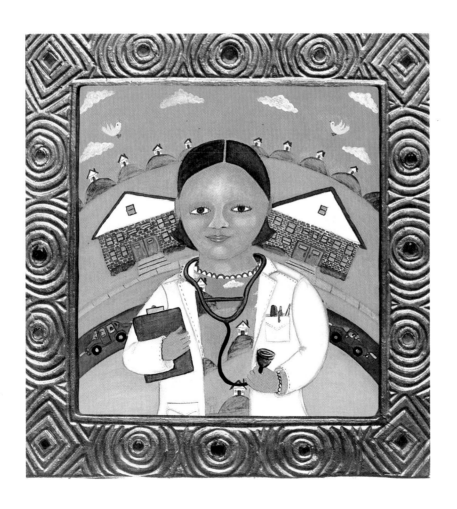

But remember this:
Joys are the same,
and love is the same.
Pain is the same,
and blood is the same.

Smiles are the same,
and hearts are just the same—
wherever they are,
wherever you are,
wherever we are,
all over the world.

Tsimshian Carver

By Diane Hoyt-Goldsmith

My name is David. My father is an artist, a woodcarver. Ever since I was little, I have watched him take a piece of wood and carve a creature from it.

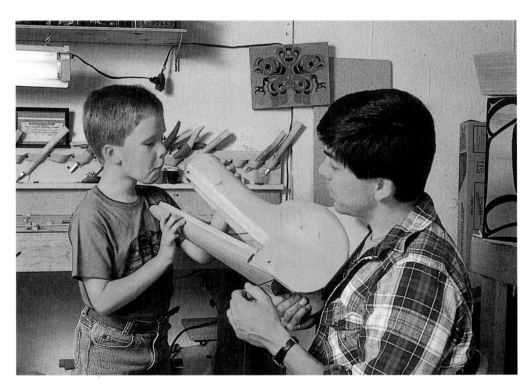

David's father shows him a wolf mask he has carved.

The cedar box David's father uses for his tools. His great-great grandfather used it as a storage box for food.

The "regalia" or button blanket that shows the eagle crest of David's people.

My father was raised in the old ways of the Tsimshian people. He learned how to fish, to hunt, and to carve. He teaches me about Tsimshian songs, dances, and legends.

My father carves totem poles. He says that a totem pole is like a signboard. He tells me it is a way to pass on legends and stories from one generation to another.

David's father looks for a cedar tree to make a totem pole.

Totem poles are made from cedar logs. The wood is soft and easy to carve.

David and his father check the carving.

Using many different tools, my father cuts into the wood where the figure he is carving is hidden. He tells me he is uncovering the spirit which is hidden in the wood. He says it is a spirit only he can see.

In the old days, carvers had special songs to chant while they worked. Now my father likes to work to songs on the radio.

David paints the eye shape.

Fine details are carved into the pole.

Now the totem pole is done. In the forest it was a beautiful tree. Then my Father saw in it the shapes of Thunderbird, Raven, Whale, and Bear. He brought them to life with his skill. I am proud to be the son of a Tsimshian carver.

Computers at Work

By Susan Green

We use computers at school
and at home. We use them to work,
to look for information, to send
e-mail, or to play games.

Jackie was going to a new school. She used
a computer to write about herself and
to draw a picture.

Here is what Jackie did.

First, I clicked on the letter icon. I used this writing tool to tell about myself. When I was done, I saved the story in a file.

Then I drew a picture of myself. To do this I clicked on the rectangle icon to make a frame.

Next I clicked on the circle icon to draw my face.

I clicked on the pencil icon and used the drawing tool to draw my nose, mouth, eyes, and hair.

When I clicked on the paintbrush icon, I coloured my hair.

I saved my picture as a file, too.

When I was finished, I showed my story to my new friends. The computer was a fun way to tell about me.

A Supermarket Song

By Bobbi Katz

Super-duper-supermarket!
We zig-zag down the aisles,
choosing veggies, fruits and eggs
from bins and stacked-up piles.
Milk and butter—cheese and cream
are in the dairy case.
There must be a thousand things,
and each has its own place.

Bottles, boxes, cans stand tall
on shelves for all to see.
"Buy me! Try me! Take me home!"
they seem to say to me!

The "Quiet" Rule

By Susan Green

Mom likes to watch mystery shows on TV. Every Tuesday night she watches "The Smart Detective." My dad and my sister and I have to be quiet.

Mom says she wants to be able to hear a pin drop. Do you know how hard it is to be *that* quiet?

My family wasn't very good at it. That's when Mom decided we needed a "quiet" rule. Every time someone made noise during the show, they had to put a dime in a special jar.

My sister liked to cause trouble. One Tuesday night she toddled over to the jar and put in a button she found on the rug.

Mom got really mad and called Dad and me into the room. Dad took the jar over to Mom, but she didn't think that was very funny.

"Dime, please," said Dad.

Plunk!

Dad and I laughed—quietly.

Who left that button where the baby could find it?!

I watched Mom while the show was on. It must have been good. Mom was on the edge of the sofa. The Smart Detective was about to solve the case.

"Oh no!" Mom groaned. A commercial came on about soap. "The commercial always comes right at the best part!"

I looked at the TV. Another commercial came on. "You know, Dad, these commercials really are a pain."

My sister toddled over to me with the jar. I dug deep into my pocket. I found an old piece of gum and a nickel.

Plunk!

Mom and I watched the rest of "The Smart Detective" together. When it was over, there was sixty-five cents in the jar. Sixty cents from Mom and a nickel from me.

I gave the money back to Mom. "You'll probably need this next Tuesday."

Just then, Dad came into the room with Emma. They did their own commercial.

Mom and I laughed. That was the best commercial we'd seen all night.

Canada's Creatures

By Susan Hughes

THE MOOSE

Its home in Canada

The moose lives all across the southern half of Canada. It can be found as far north as the Northwest Territories and parts of the Yukon.

Take a look

Moose are usually dark brown or black. A male moose weighs about 635 kilograms—about the same weight as 8 full-grown men. It has large antlers made of solid bone.

On the move

Moose always live near water. They are great swimmers! Baby moose can swim when they are only a few weeks old. Moose head to the water to escape from insects and summer heat. They eat underwater plants and leaves, twigs, and bark from trees that grow near water.

Keeping track

Moose tracks are about 13 cm wide and heart-shaped.

Record-breaking fact
The moose is the largest member of the deer family in the world!

THE MOUNTAIN LION

Its home in Canada

Mountain lions used to live across Canada.
Now there are not many left in eastern Canada.
Most Canadian mountain lions are found in
British Columbia and Alberta.

Take a look

The mountain lion is a big cat! Its body is usually brown or grey, and it has a white chest and throat.

On the move

Mountain lions live in forests, grasslands, or mountains. They hunt at night. Mountain lions are expert jumpers and climbers. Sometimes a mountain lion will sneak up on its prey. Sometimes it will wait in a tree above a trail for hours. When a deer, elk, or moose passes by, it drops onto its back. Mountain lions will also hunt porcupines, beavers, mice, squirrels, and other small mammals.

Name that cat!

The mountain lion is also known as a puma, cougar, painter, catamount, and panther.

THE COMMON LOON

Its home in Canada

The common loon can be found across Canada. There are not as many now as there used to be. People are trying to find ways to keep Canada's lakes home to the loon.

Take a look

The common loon has a black head. Its back is checkered black and white. It has a white belly and a white bar across its throat.

On the move

Loons eat fish, frogs, and even ducks! The legs of loons are placed far back on their body. This makes them powerful swimmers. It also makes it difficult for them to move on land. This is why loons build their nests right at the edge of the water. This way they can slip into the water quickly if danger threatens!

Call of the wild

The call of a loon can sound like a wolf's wail or an eerie yodel.

THE BLACK BEAR

Its home in Canada

Black bears can be found across Canada. They are the most common of North American bears.

Take a look

Black bears come in many different colours: black, brown, sometimes almost white! Male black bears can weigh as much as two full-grown men, about 170 kilograms. Bears sleep during the winter months. When they wake up, they are very hungry!

On the move

Black bears are experts at climbing trees. They do this to escape danger or to look for food. The black bear eats plants, roots, grains, nuts, and berries. Of course, it also loves honey—and it will even eat the bees, too!

Keeping track

The black bear puts its whole foot on the ground when it walks, even its five toes and its heel.

The Paper Crane

By Molly Bang

A man once owned a restaurant on a
busy road. He loved to cook good food
and he loved to serve it. He worked from
morning until night, and he was happy.

But a new highway was built close by.
Travellers drove straight from one place
to another and no longer stopped at the
restaurant. Many days went by when no
guests came at all. The man became very
poor, and had nothing to do but dust and
polish his empty plates and tables.

One evening a stranger came into the restaurant. His clothes were old and worn, but he had an unusual, gentle manner.

Though he said he had no money to pay for food, the owner invited him to sit down. He cooked the best meal he could make and served him like a king.

When the stranger had finished, he said to his host, "I cannot pay you with money, but I would like to thank you in my own way."

He picked up a paper napkin from the table and folded it into the shape of a crane. "You have only to clap your hands," he said, "and this bird will come to life and dance for you. Take it, and enjoy it while it is with you." With these words the stranger left.

It happened just as the stranger had said. The owner had only to clap his hands and the paper crane became a living bird, flew down to the floor, and danced.

Soon word of the dancing crane spread, and people came from far and near to see the magic bird perform.

The owner was happy again, for his restaurant was always full of guests.

He cooked and served and had company from morning until night.

The weeks passed.

And the months.

One evening a man came into the restaurant. His clothes were old and worn, but he had an unusual, gentle manner. The owner knew him at once and was overjoyed.

The stranger, however, said nothing. He took a flute from his pocket, raised it to his lips, and began to play.

The crane flew down from its place on the shelf and danced as it had never danced before.

The stranger finished playing, lowered the flute from his lips, and returned it to his pocket. He climbed on the back of the crane, and they flew out of the door and away.

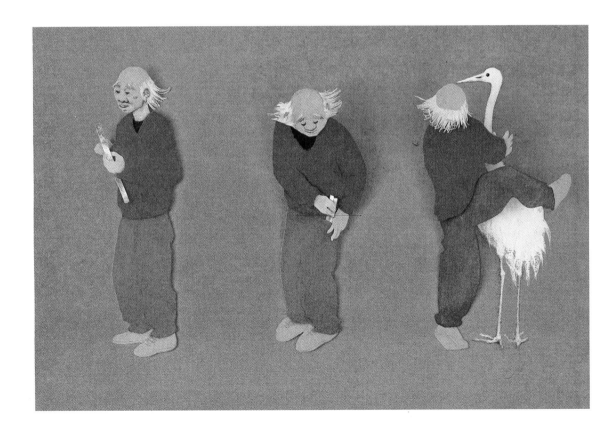

The restaurant still stands by the side of the road, and guests still come to eat the good food and hear the story of the gentle stranger and the magic crane made from a paper napkin. But neither the stranger nor the dancing crane has ever been seen again.

Sidewalk Sticks

By Marie E. Cecchini

Here's a recipe for homemade sidewalk chalk that's as much fun to make as it is to use.

What You'll Need:

8 white eggshells
20 mL hot water
red, yellow, and blue food
  colouring
20 mL flour
dish
small bowl
wire whisk
spatula
foil

What to Do:

1. Carefully clean and dry eggshells. Place a few shells at a time in a dish and grind them into powder. It may take a few minutes to grind eggshells completely.

2. Put 5 mL of hot water into small bowl. Add 1 or 2 drops of food colouring. If you want red, yellow, or blue chalk, use 2 drops of that colour. For purple chalk, use 1 drop red and 1 drop blue. For green, use 1 drop blue and 1 drop yellow. For orange, use 1 drop red and 1 drop yellow.

3. Add 5 mL flour to water and food colouring and stir well with whisk.

4. Add 15 mL of the eggshell powder and stir with whisk until mixture is well blended and sticky.

5. Use spatula to scrape mixture out of bowl and into your hands. Firmly shape the mixture into a stick. Set finished stick on a piece of foil to dry. Thoroughly rinse and dry bowl.

Repeat steps 2 through 5 until you have four chalk sticks.

Your chalk will take
two or three days to dry
once you've shaped it.
When it's dry, you can use
it to create a sidewalk
mural or play hopscotch or
tick-tack-toe with a friend.
Whatever you draw will
disappear with the next
rain shower, and then
you can draw again!

Mary Margaret's Tree

By Blair Drawson

It was spring, and Mary Margaret
had a tree to plant.

Down in the garden, she dug a hole.

She turned up several stones,
some tin cans,
two rusty nails,
and an old bone.

Digging was hard work.

By the time she was finished,
Mary Margaret was quite tired.

For some reason, she also
felt rather small.
What on earth?
She was shrinking!

But the tree took root
and sprouted many leaves,
and grew to become tall
and magnificent.

Gathering her courage,
Mary Margaret climbed the mighty trunk.

It was green,
green,
green among the leaves!

She made her way to the top of a tall branch.

It was a wonderful thing
to see the world from on high.

Birds flew back and forth,
busily building nests.
Strange insects chirped and fluttered,
chattering in all directions.

Mary Margaret felt snug and happy
inside a large white flower.

"How perfectly lovely," she sighed.

Eggs hatched, and soon the
air was filled with the sound
of peeping baby birds.
They wanted food!

Mary Margaret was glad
that she did not have to eat
a worm.

At night, the sky was full of
bright stars and fireflies.

Moths and hooting owls flew around the moon.

One day there came a flapping of wings, and the flower bobbed up and down fearfully.
A huge, hungry woodpecker!
Did it think she was a bug?
Happily, the bird soon realized his mistake, and was gone.

Now summer was coming to an end.
The days were getting shorter,
and the nights cooler.
Fall was coming. The leaves were
turning colour.
It was time for them to go.

Suddenly, a great gust of wind came
up, and Mary Margaret grabbed a
leaf just in time.

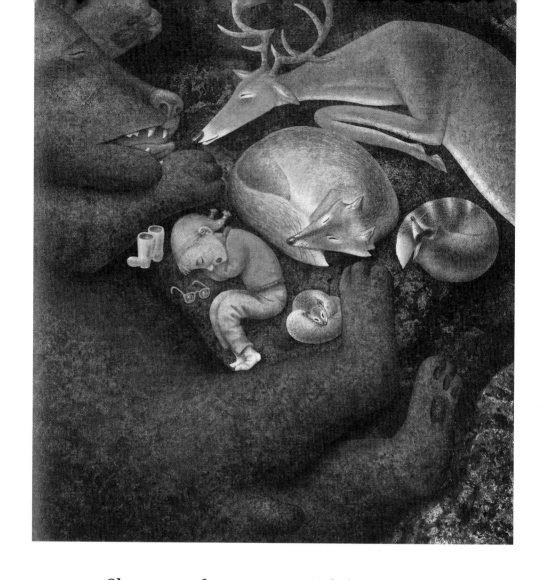

She went for a crazy ride!

By chance she flew into a cave.
It was home to some hibernating
animals.

There she spent the winter in a
deep, peaceful sleep.

Spring arrived at last, and Mary
Margaret awoke from her slumber.
She began to feel a strange sensation.
Her feet grew roots, and her fingers
sent out little green shoots.
Leaves began to appear.

"How very unusual," said Mary Margaret.

Soon there was a brand-new tree, and the tree was Mary Margaret.

"Mary Margaret, where are you?"

She was being called.

"Come in for dinner now, dear," said her mother. "You must be hungry."

And Mary Margaret decided that she really was very hungry indeed.

Acknowledgments

Permission to reprint copyrighted material is gratefully acknowledged. Every effort has been made to trace ownership of all copyrighted material and to secure permission from copyright holders. In the event of any question arising as to the use of any material, we will be pleased to make the necessary corrections in future printings.

"Visiting Aunt Zelda" first appeared in SPIDER magazine, April 1998. Copyright © Jeanne Modesitt. Reprinted with permission of the author. "A List" from FROG AND TOAD TOGETHER copyright © 1971, 1972 by Arnold Lobel. Used by permission of HarperCollins Publishers. "How to Be a Friend" by Pat Lowery Collins from You and Me. Text copyright © 1997 by Pat Lowery Collins, poet, author and artist. Reprinted with permission of the author. Illustration copyright © 1997 by Sally Mavor. Used with permission of Orchard Books. "I Have a Friend" by Karla Kuskin from You and Me. Text used with permission. Illustration copyright © 1997 by Sally Mavor. Used with permission of Orchard Books. "The Enormous Potato" by Aubrey Davis, illustrated by Dusan Petricic, used by permission of Kids Can Press Ltd., Toronto. Text copyright © 1997 by Aubrey Davis. Illustrations copyright © 1997 by Dusan Petricic. "Whoever You Are" © 1997 by Mem Fox. Illustration © 1997 by Leslie Staub. Reprinted by permission of Harcourt Brace & Co. "Totem Poles" adapted from TOTEM POLE by Diane Hoyt-Goldsmith. Photographs copyright © 1990 by Lawrence Migdale. All rights reserved. Used by permission of Holiday House, Inc. "All About Me" by Susan Green © 1999 ITP Nelson. "A Supermarket Song" copyright © 1991 by Bobbi Katz. Reprinted with permission of the author who controls all rights. "The "Quiet" Rule" by Susan Green © 1999 ITP Nelson. "Canada's Creatures" by Susan Hughes © 1999 ITP Nelson. "The Paper Crane" used by permission of Greenwillow Books, a division of William Morrow & Company. Text copyright © 1985 by Molly Garrett Bang. "Sidewalk Sticks" by Marie E. Cecchini—Reprinted by permission of SPIDER magazine, July 1998, Vol. 5, No. 7. © 1998 by Carus Publishing Company. Mary Margaret's Tree copyright © 1996 by Blair Drawson. A Groundwood Book/Douglas & McIntyre.

Illustrations

Cover: Tony Goffe; pp. 4-7 Marie-Claude Favreau; pp. 8-13, 15-21 Arnold Lobel; pp. 22-23 Sally Mavor; pp. 24-35 Dusan Petricic; pp. 37-43 Leslie Staub; pp. 52-54 William Kimber; p. 57 Scot Ritchie; pp. 59-63 Capucine Mazille; pp. 65, 67, 69-71 Jack McMaster; pp. 81-83 Stephanie Roth; pp. 84, 86-88, 90, 92-95 Blair Drawson.

Photographs

pp. 44-49 © Lawrence Migdale; p. 50 photo courtesy of Anglican Foundation; pp. 51-55 Dave Starrett; p. 64 © Corel Corporation; p. 66 © PhotoDisc, Inc.; p. 68 © Corel Corporation; p. 71 © PhotoDisc, Inc.